LEGENDS
and
TRADITIONS
of
CHRISTMAS

D0249070

LEGENDS
and
TRADITIONS
of
CHRISTMAS

Devotional Ideas for Family and Group Use During Advent

TRUDIE WEST REVOIR

Illustrated by
SHIRLEY A. SPENCER

Judson Press ® Valley Forge

LEGENDS AND TRADITIONS OF CHRISTMAS
Copyright © 1985
Judson Press, Valley Forge, PA 19482-0851
Third Printing, 1989

All rights reserved. No part of this publication may be reproduced, stored in a retrieval system, or transmitted in any form or by any means, electronic, mechanical, photocopying, recording, or otherwise, without the prior permission of the copyright owner, except for brief quotations included in a review of the book.

Library of Congress Cataloging in Publication Data
Revoir, Trudie West.
  Legends and traditions of Christmas.
  "Devotional ideas for family and group use during Advent."
  Bibliography: p.
  1. Christmas—Meditations.   2. Advent.   I. Title.
BV45.R47   1985   394.2'68282   85-5582
ISBN 0-8170-1082-3

The name JUDSON PRESS is registered as a trademark in the U.S. Patent Office.
Printed in the U.S.A.

To my beloved great-grandchildren,

Brian	Sean	Fawn	Carmen
Cheneene	Shane and Tory	Trinity	Grayson

and to all other boys and girls who find it hard to wait
with patience for Christmas Day.

Acknowledgments

There are many, many people who should be thanked for helping me in the writing of this book. It has been "in process" for so many years, however, that it is not now possible to remember all those who whetted my appetite, instructed me in, and delighted me with Christmas legends. Yet these persons are a part of me and a part of this work. I would especially like to give credit and my heartfelt thanks to the following persons.

For suggestions in the use of legends in devotional material:
Miss Hazel McAfee, Tampa, Florida
Miss Anne Sinclair, Winnipeg, Manitoba, Canada
Mrs. James Green (my niece, 'Cilla), Escanaba, Michigan.

I owe many happy hours to Mrs. Mary Harper, who saved for me every Christmas card or article that came her way which contained a legend.

All of the churches with whom I have worked and all of the students whom I have taught in college and seminary have added their share of information about Christmas legends.

From my mother and my "second mother" I inherited copious files of church teaching material.

And to Mrs. Shirley Spencer, the interesting, congenial, and talented young mother who has drawn the illustrations and was so much fun to know and work with, I owe shared joy of creativity and completion.

Foreword

Legends and Traditions of Christmas is not intended to be an academic study or an encyclopedia of Christmas legends. Because there are many variations in the content of legendary literature, there are many more legends than can possibly be included in a book of this size. I have discovered luscious bits of fact and fiction which are interesting to know but are extraneous to the purpose of this book. I have also learned of many methods for marking the beginning of Advent which are correct, but may be more confusing to compute. And only one is needed.

Rather than a comprehensive volume of legends, my book is for the enjoyment of elementary school age children. I have striven for simplicity in vocabulary and meaning. However, people of all ages enjoy legends so I have also included an appendix listing various uses for the book.

I hope that this book will provide inspiration and enjoyment to children and others who also delight in the things that delight children. It represents a rich heritage that I have spent a lifetime discovering!

Contents

Introduction

Ever since the Middle Ages, the weeks preceding Christmas have been called "Advent." The word means "coming," and refers to a period of preparation for the birth of Jesus. In the tradition of the church it is a time of penitence and of spiritual searching, so that if the Christ child should knock at the door of my heart on Christmas Eve, I should be ready to receive him and not say, "There is no room!"

Christmas is a whole season, not just a day. Advent can be a very long time for children who see, hear, and feel all the preparation going on around them. They can do little to participate, and since they have no concept of time, the waiting is not easy. Using an Advent calendar is a fun way to help a young child, or any of us, to count the days until Christmas and ease the impatience.

The simplest and most visual form of Advent calendar for the *very* young is a colored paper chain which has rings for every day in Advent. As the child removes one ring each day, he or she can see that Christmas is coming nearer, and when the whole chain is gone it will be Christmas Day.

Swedish families have long used an Advent calendar made like a pretty Christmas picture. Each day one small shutter on the picture is opened, revealing a miniature view or verse inside. Most bookstores now carry Advent calendars.

This book is also an Advent calendar, combining the counting of the days with some of the legends of Christmas. A legend is a story which comes down to us from the past. It is believed to be true but there are no verifiable facts to prove it. These legends, however, are a rich Christmas heritage and are ours to know, wonder about, and enjoy.

In order to use this book as an Advent calendar, you will need to determine the number of days in Advent (see pages 16-17) and choose the correct number of stories to read. After you have chosen which legends you will use, you can mark the days in Advent by reading one story each day. You will read the last story on Christmas Eve. It has been almost two thousand years since the birth of Jesus, and many stories and traditions have developed during this time. Some of the legends do not sound as if they really could have happened, but nevertheless they can teach us lessons in thoughtfulness, kindness, and generosity. Some of them may be founded on actual events. You will have fun deciding for yourselves which ones really happened and which ones didn't.

In this country, our Christmas pictures show the shepherds, angels, and wise men gathered around the manger. This is usually how we reenact the Christmas story and is reflected in the carols we sing. It leads us to believe that the shepherds, angels, and wise men were all present on Christmas Eve. However, it is believed that the visit of the wise men took place at a later date and that they probably worshiped baby Jesus in a house which Joseph had found for himself and his family to stay in until Mary and the Baby were strong enough for the long journey back to Nazareth. January 6, called "The Feast of Epiphany," is the day the church has set aside to celebrate the coming of the wise men. It completes the "Twelve Days of Christmas."

Some of the legends are about the people and animals that gathered around the manger when Jesus was born; some are about the gift-bearers, based on the story of the wise men bringing their gifts; and some relate to the flight of Mary, Joseph, and the Baby to Egypt.

The four Sundays of Advent are very special Sundays. Devotions for these Sundays are included in this book. You might like to make an Advent wreath with five candles (four for the Sundays and one for Jesus) and light one each Sunday as you read the devotion for that day. Light the Christ candle on Christmas Eve (after reading the final legend) or on Christmas morning (before opening gifts) to celebrate the birth of Jesus, "the light of the world." Since I hope you will use this book year after year, I have not put dates or days on the pages of the stories except for the Sundays.

The early church did not celebrate the birth of Jesus. The church observed his baptism, crucifixion, and resurrection. They celebrated his baptism on January 6, but it was some time before they settled on that date to remember his birth as well, because when times of persecution came, it seemed unwise for Christians to attract attention to themselves by celebrating a special day for Christ's birth.

December 25 was already part of a great holiday in the Roman Empire. This date roughly corresponded with the Solstice, marking the time when the sun began to set a little later each day. Since light was coming back to the world and since Jesus was "the light of the world" for Christians, it seemed a good time to commemorate his birthday. Many pagans who were becoming Christians were already used to this holiday. They also had a great celebration called "Saturnalia" at this time. And so, as far as we know, more than three hundred years after the birth of Jesus, the church held its first Christmas Day on December 25 in the year A.D. 336.

We can find the basis for some of our treasured traditions in the pagan festival of Saturnalia. The Roman celebration included lighting lights, giving gifts to the poor, and taking live branches to friends as symbols of health and happiness. It was easy to associate this with the three kings bearing gifts to the Christ child. In some of the other legends you will also find customs from pagan backgrounds which entered the Christian festival of Christmas, and they have become beautiful symbols of our faith.

William Sansom, in A Book of Christmas,[1] states that our American Christmas is especially rich today because the immigrants carried hundreds of ancient customs to their new land. Coming from almost every country in the world, these people brought with them customs and legends of their own national celebrations of Christmas. All of these traditions have been melded

[1] William Sansom, A Book of Christmas (New York: McGraw Hill, 1968), p. 90.

into a festival season which holds out love and acceptance to everyone. We are all richer and more understanding when we know these lovely stories.

Make sure that children do not become confused between the biblical stories which provide the background for Christmas and these pretty legends which, although they are probably not true, do have a lesson of love, kindness, and unselfishness to share with us.

There seems to be no age limit to the enjoyment of legends. May they enrich your life as they have mine.

Information about the Calendar of Advent

The period of Advent can vary from twenty-two to twenty-eight days. Advent will always begin on the first Sunday after November 26, with the earliest possible beginning being November 27 and the latest possible beginning being December 3.

Because I wanted to provide enough legends for the longest Advent season, I have included twenty-eight days in the calendar booklet. Therefore, there will be too many pages for some of the years. Before you begin to use this book, especially if you are reading it to children, count the number of days in the current Advent season. It may be necessary to leave out a few of the legends or occasionally read two stories so that you complete the booklet on Christmas Eve.

It will be meaningful if you make a special effort to read all of the Gospel readings which are included for each of the Sundays of Advent because they include the real Christmas stories from Matthew and Luke. December 6 is the special feast day for honoring Saint Nicholas and December 13 is the day when Santa Lucia goes around her house in Sweden, wearing a crown of lighted candles and singing to her family. If you want to read those legends on those special days, you must plan ahead carefully.

The following calendar will help you know how many days there will be in Advent for the next several years. If you plan your readings with the right number of days in mind, you will finish on Christmas Eve.

1989 — 22 days

1990 — 23 days

1991 — 24 days

1992 — 26 days

1993 — 27 days		1997 — 25 days
1994 — 28 days		1998 — 26 days
1995 — 22 days		1999 — 27 days
1996 — 24 days		2000 — 22 days

Introduction to the Four Sundays of Advent

Separate and ide [handwritten note]

During these next four Sundays you will be trying to prepare your heart for the coming of the Christ child. It doesn't matter whether you have a big family or a small family or are completely alone. Before you begin to use this book, you may want to make a special place for worship in your home where you can sit down, read, meditate, talk, and sing. Try singing and reading out loud—it's exciting! You can gather and place the following items on a table or shelf: one of your favorite Christmas pictures; a Bible, open to the Nativity stories; and some greens and holly. Arrange the whole setting as creatively as you can. This can become your worship center.

If you do not already have an Advent wreath, you can easily make one. It should have greenery and five candles. One candle, which represents Christ, will be taller than the others. Advent candles are usually purple, denoting penitence and royalty. But the central Christ candle is white, standing for the purity of Jesus, the "light of the world." Five votive candles in holders are safer when you use live greens, or you can bore five candle holes in a thick, round board, decorating between the candles with holly and fir.

You may want to look through the legends in advance to ascertain which figures will be needed for each program. Each week you can add the figures suggested in each of the Sunday devotions to the worship place. If you do, they will all be assembled by Christmas. We know the events in the Christmas story probably didn't all happen before Christmas Day. However, we want to tell the complete Bible events as well as the mystical legends which we enjoy.

Try to be prepared before you begin the little service by having the Nativity figurines in your lap, the picture ready, the Bible with its place all marked, and the matches at hand. Children like to take part in reading, singing, and fixing up the altar.

First Sunday in Advent— The Annunciation

A Service for "The Candle of Waiting"

Now take the little figures of the angel and Mary that you are holding and place them on your worship table or wherever you plan to create your Nativity scene. If you don't have figures of the angel and Mary, you can use a picture of the Annunciation instead. Or you can use both, if you like.

Sing: "Watchman, Tell Us of the Night" or another carol. If you can't sing alone, try reading the words aloud.

Read the Bible Story: Luke 1:26-33 and 46-49.

When we have birthdays, we light candles. So, for the birthday of Christ we celebrate with candles and lights. We have lights on our Christmas trees, the light from our Yule log fire, and candles in the windows. We remember that Jesus said, "I am the light of the world" (John 8:12).

Let us think about how long families have to wait before a baby can be born. Grandmothers and grandfathers, aunts and uncles, fathers and mothers, sisters and brothers, and sometimes even friends and neighbors are all waiting, hoping, and dreaming. That is the way your parents waited for you and how Jesus' father and mother, Joseph and Mary, waited for him. Let us think about this as we light the first candle of Advent, "The Candle of Waiting."

Prayer: "Dear God, who sent us the Christmas Baby, the happy season of Advent has come again. As we lighted the First Advent Candle, we thought of the long months our parents waited for us to be born and Mary and Joseph waited for the

Christ child. As we plan the gifts we are going to give, help us to be sure that they are gifts full of love. Help us to make or buy presents that will make people happy. And if the gifts we give are small, help our family and friends to know that our love is big because we are remembering that the birth of Jesus was the sign of God's love to all of us. Amen."

Sing: "O Come, O Come, Emmanuel" or some other favorite carol.

Legend of
The Holly Wreath

After "the angels were gone away from them into heaven" (Luke 2:15), the excited shepherds all began talking at once. They shouted to each other across the fields. "Who will watch the sheep while we go see the baby Jesus?" "Who will lead the group to find the stable?" "What gift can we take to Jesus?"

One little boy who was very small and very poor was with the group, learning how to be a shepherd. He didn't have any family or any home, so he stayed with the sheep all day and all night. Some of the older shepherds would take him home with them for a visit and sometimes they gave him part of their food. They were kindly men and when his old robe wore out they found him another one.

This Little Shepherd knew he wouldn't be asked to go with the first group to see baby Jesus, but he didn't mind that. He could wait. But when he heard the men talking about their gifts he was worried.

"I'm going to take him this perfect little pet lamb; the boy and the lamb can grow up together!"

"I'll take him this flute I carved last winter; it's the best one I ever made."

"I have three pieces of shiny, silver money tucked in my belt—I'll give that to him."

"I think I'll stop at my house on the way and get a lovely jug that my wife made. He would like that, I'm sure."

The Little Shepherd thought about all these gifts as the shepherds left for Bethlehem. He knew he would go with the second group to see Jesus, and he wondered and wondered what he could take to the manger child.

As the dawn began to send the long rays of the sun across the field, it lighted up a beautiful bush of holly. "Oh, I know! I'll make a royal crown for the Baby," thought the Little Shepherd. He broke off the most tender branches and carefully wove them into a neat circle. It looked very pretty—but it did not look like a crown for a baby king, and he almost threw it away, but when his turn came to go and see the baby, he picked it up because he had nothing else to give.

The second group of shepherds entered the stable quietly and curiously. There was the Christ child, "wrapped in swaddling clothes and lying in a manger" (Luke 2:12), just as the angel had said. Even the oldest shepherds were awed, and fell down on their knees and worshiped him. They presented their gifts to the baby Jesus, who was sleeping, as most new babies do.

The Little Shepherd knew that it was time for him to lay his gift beside the others. As he put his crown of holly branches down among all of the precious gifts, it looked so poor that he began to cry. He really wished he had something nice to give that beautiful Baby!

Then the Christ child opened his eyes and smiled at the Little Shepherd. Jesus reached out his hand and touched the holly crown and suddenly the leaves glistened with a bright, shiny greenness and the Little Shepherd's teardrops turned into scarlet berries! It looked like a royal crown, fit for a tiny king! And the Little Shepherd and the baby Jesus smiled happily into each others' eyes.

That is why, through all the years, holly wreaths have become a traditional Christmas decoration. We hang them on doors, over fireplaces, and even in our windows to remind us of Christ the King and the miracle of the little crown of holly.

Legend of
The Robin

On the rafters in a stable in the little town of Bethlehem, there perched a Little Brown Bird. With her bright eyes she watched the people who had come from many lands. She saw them place their gifts before the dear little Baby who was wrapped tightly in swaddling clothes and lying in a manger bed. The adoration and love on the faces of the kneeling people made her feel that something great and holy was taking place.

The Little Brown Bird watched from her high perch all day long. Sometimes she fluttered from one beam to another in order to see everything better, but she didn't make a sound nor did she come down from the rafters to get in anyone's way.

When evening came, all the visitors went home. The holy family settled down to sleep at last. The day's excitement had made them very tired. The Little Brown Bird flew down and perched on the edge of the manger. She wanted to get a closer look at the Christ child. She looked and looked with her bright little eyes and when she had seen everything, she flew back to the rafters and tucked her beak under her wing in preparation to go to sleep.

Just as she was dozing off, she noticed that the fire was going out. She had watched, earlier, as Joseph had built up the fire to warm the Baby through the night. She looked over at Joseph, but he was snoring soundly. Mary, the mother, was gently sleeping, too.

The Little Brown Bird flew down from her perch and began

fanning the fire with her wings. At first she thought the fire was dead, but gradually, as she fanned and fanned it, she saw it spark and grow brighter again. In the firelight the feathers on the Little Brown Bird's breast began to glow and shine a beautiful red.

The Little Brown Bird stayed by the fire all night long. She grew terribly sleepy and nearly fell into the fire once or twice, but she fanned the blaze to keep the Christ child warm until morning came. Since that night the robin's breast has always been a warm flame color, a symbol of the bird's love for the Baby in the manger, Jesus Christ, our Savior.

Legend of
The Yule Log

On that wondrous Christmas Eve so long ago, the shepherds were sitting around their cheery campfires on the hillside. They were singing and telling stories.

"That's enough for tonight," Jonathan said. "Let's get some sleep." So they lay down beside the warm embers and fell asleep.

Then a great choir of angel voices woke them up with a start! You can imagine how frightened and excited the shepherds must have been!

When the voices were gone and the brilliance had faded from the sky, the shepherds wrapped their warm cloaks around them and hurried to Bethlehem. They found the baby Jesus in the manger, just as the angels had told them they would. They knelt down and worshiped him.

When they stood up to leave, they noticed the coolness of the stable. There wasn't any fire to warm the chill night air.

Fourteen-year-old Asa was the youngest of the shepherds. His father was called "Big Asa."

"Go out and find some wood, Asa, if you please, and build a little fire to warm the Baby," suggested Big Asa.

Asa went out and gathered an armload of dead branches from under an ash tree. He came back inside the stable and made a nice fire for the little family. Then he brought an extra pile of wood and laid it beside the manger. After Joseph had thanked him, the shepherds went back to their flocks.

Perhaps that was the beginning of our Christmas fire traditions; no one really knows. There are other stories, too.

Many hundreds of years ago the people of Norway and Denmark built great bonfires when they noticed that the sun was staying away a little longer every day in the late fall. They thought their fires would give the sun new life and strength. They probably brought their custom to Britain with them when they came as fierce Viking warriors to conquer the land.

In almost every European country this same celebration was used to try to give new life to the dying sun. Usually the people threw a green branch on the logs, poured wine over the whole thing, and then lit it with a piece of wood that had been saved from the previous year's ceremony.

In the great castles of Britain everyone gathered to celebrate Christmas for two weeks. The very beginning of the festival was marked by the lighting of the Yule log on Christmas Eve. The lords and ladies invited all of their relatives, friends, farm workers, soldiers, and servants to witness this event. They streamed into the great hall of the castle. It was like a wonderful party!

When everyone was ready, strong young men took hold of the heavy ropes attached to the log. They pulled, groaned, and tugged until the great Yule log had been dragged the length of the hall and set in place. Sometimes the log was the whole trunk of a tree, but it could fit in the hearth because their fireplaces were higher than a man and half as wide as the wall.

Then the lord of the castle took the piece of wood he had saved from the fire of the previous Christmas, lit it, and then lit the twigs and kindling under the Yule log. The flames leaped high and all of the people cheered and cheered!

When the fire was burning steadily, everyone walked past it in single file. They play-acted throwing all of their old hates and quarrels into the flames. This symbolized that they were forgiving one another for everything mean or unkind from the past year and starting the new celebration with love and peace in their hearts.

Legend of
The Lamb's Woolly Coat

BaBa was a little lamb who had a rough, shaggy coat to keep her warm. She lived in a stable with a big, brown cow and a little gray donkey.

BaBa was only a little lamb and she was sound asleep when the Christ child was born and wrapped in a cloth and laid to sleep on the hay. When the shepherds came seeking the Babe in the manger, the stable shone with a mystical light. BaBa awoke and stared and listened.

Even though she felt very much afraid, she crept a little nearer. She heard what the shepherds said to Mary, the Baby's mother. BaBa watched them kneel down and worship the Baby. She saw them giving their beautiful lambs to Joseph and then she heard them singing all the way back to the fields outside of town. She noticed how Joseph and Mary smiled curiously at each other as they settled down again to sleep. They were very tired.

BaBa watched the Baby for a while. "He must be a very special child," she thought, "to get all this attention." Ever so softly she crept near and watched him while he slept. Once he opened his eyes and whimpered a little. BaBa whispered softly, "Go back to sleep, little wonder Baby!" BaBa noticed how ragged and old the blanket was that was wrapped around the Baby and what a thin, little bit of hay he had under him. The Baby shivered and whimpered again.

"Why, he's cold!" BaBa thought in surprise. She snuggled right up close and curled herself around the baby Jesus. Soon

Jesus felt warm and happy. He smiled at BaBa and touched her rough, shaggy coat with his tiny hand as if to say, "Thank you, BaBa!"

And suddenly BaBa's rough coat was changed into a lovely, soft, curly wool coat—right then and there! Ever since that night all sheep have had soft, warm, curly woolen coats.

Legend of Babushka

If you were a Russian child today, you would hardly know what to believe about Christmas. When your great-grandmother was a little girl, she had several gift-givers to dream about. There was "Father Christmas" who came on Christmas Eve in some parts of the country. In other places they believed that a white-robed maiden named "Kolyäda" (meaning "Christmas") came on Christmas Eve. Kolyäda went from house to house, riding in a beautiful white sleigh. People went with her and sang carols. Instead of leaving gifts for the children, people gave Kolyäda small presents and treats. Then on January 6, which was Epiphany, "Babushka" gave the children gifts.

Ever since the Russians had a revolution, children have been told that they must forget about Father Christmas, Kolyäda, and even their favorite, Babushka, because these legendary figures were based on the Bible Christmas stories. Instead, Russian children are taught to look for Grandfather Frost to bring them gifts on New Year's Day, which is not a religious holiday. Grandfather Frost is an old man who sometimes dresses in winter furs like Santa Claus, or sometimes wears a long, red bishop's robe. But the Russian people know he is not a religious figure.

I imagine, though, that when children sit around the fire at holiday time and their grandparents tell them stories about when *they* were children, some grandmothers and grandfathers still tell them the story of old Babushka. It is one of their oldest and best loved legends. Perhaps the elderly storyteller has to say to the children, "Now, of course, you know this story isn't true; it is just a legend."

Babushka (which means "grandmother") sat beside her nice warm fire, dreaming about her tasty supper that was bubbling away in the iron pot, and about her cozy, warm bed. Suddenly there was a sharp knock at the door. She opened it and there stood a group of shepherds.

"Grandmother," the leader told her, "a wonderful thing has happened. Come with us to Bethlehem and see the Little King. Come and bring a present!"

Old Babushka felt the cold, frosty air coming through the door and she shivered. She hadn't eaten her supper yet and she wanted her own warm bed.

"I am too old," she whispered, "too old to be out in the frosty night air. I will go in the morning." And she closed the door.

But the shepherds knocked again, more loudly this time. "Grandmother, Grandmother," they insisted, "you are rich and you know how to do many things. If *you* can't go in the cold, then please pack a basket of gifts and goodies and we will take it for you."

This time the old lady didn't even go to the door. She just rocked and rocked and said to herself, "Tomorrow will be time enough."

Finally the shepherds went along without her. Babushka ate her tasty supper by the fire and went to sleep in her cozy bed.

Next morning, she packed a basketful of meat and bread, oranges and cakes. She took a soft blue shawl she had made for Mary, and a little silver spoon for the baby Jesus and left for the stable.

When Babushka came to the stable, she couldn't believe her eyes—it was empty! She asked all of the neighbors and all of the townspeople where she could find the family and she looked everywhere. But Mary and Joseph and Jesus were gone! She wept with shame because she had come too late.

Ever since then Babushka wanders about the world with her basket of gifts, through cold and snowy woods, always looking for the Christ child but never finding him. At Christmas time, whenever she comes to a house where a good child is sleeping, she leaves three gifts: one to marvel at, one to enjoy, and one for the baby Jesus.

Even though Babushka looks a bit like a wrinkled old witch, children have always loved to hear her story.

Legend of
The Christmas Rose

It seems as though our favorite Christmas flower in America is the Poinsettia. Perhaps that is because our plant scientists have learned to grow them so well, in many sizes and shades of color. They can be shipped all over the country so that people everywhere in America can enjoy them. But before the year 1850 the *real* Christmas flower was called the "Christmas Rose." There were rose farms that specialized in growing these plants.

When you think of the Christmas Rose, if you are imagining the beautiful roses that bloom in our gardens in the spring, and even in the summer and fall, you are mistaken. The true Christmas Rose is what the plant books call the "Black Hellebore," although it isn't black at all.

In places where there is snow in the winter, you probably will not be able to find a Christmas Rose. In places where it is warm enough to roller skate and play ball outside all year round, however, the Christmas Rose might begin to flower before Christmas and keep on blooming until April. The leaves are very large and dark. The bloom is a lovely, greenish white at first and then it turns purple in color. I have one in my garden.

There is a legend about the Christmas Rose that goes like this:

There was a Little Shepherdess who also came to the manger in Bethlehem to worship the baby Jesus. She looked with wide open eyes at all of the presents that other people had given him and then she started to cry, for her hands were empty.

As she cried, her tears fell on the ground around the baby

Jesus. Wherever they touched the earth, a beautiful white flower sprang up. The Little Shepherdess laughed with delight as she picked a bouquet of the blossoms. She held them out to the Christ child and knelt in adoration before his crib.

Then the Baby's tiny hand touched the flowers and on every one a delicate tinge of pink appeared. It made them even more beautiful. It was the Christ child's way of saying "Thank you for the Christmas Rose, Little Shepherdess!"

Second Sunday in Advent— The Birth of Jesus

A Service for "The Candle of Joy"

If you made a worship table in your home last week, sit near it now and enjoy it. Light again the first candle of Advent and remember what we said about the angel and Mary and the long months of waiting.

Sing: "There's a Song in the Air" or another carol you know.

Read the Bible story: Luke 2:1-7.

Now light the second Advent candle, "The Candle of Joy," and think about the joy and excitement that your family felt when you were born. We know that the tiny Baby in the manger brought love and joy to the whole world.

If you were a child in Europe, especially on a farm, you would be told that every Christmas Eve at midnight, wherever they are, in stable, field or barnyard, all the oxen, horses and sheep kneel and bow toward Bethlehem in the East. Then they sing praises to God in *human* voices! I have never seen or heard this myself, but of course, I've never been on a farm in Europe at Christmastime!

In every Catholic country people build mangers and sometimes use live animals in their Nativity scenes. Seeing the créche with Mary and Joseph and the animals standing around helps to make the Bible story come alive. Perhaps the people watching remember how tired Mary and Joseph were after their long journey from Nazareth and are glad the innkeeper said, "Come sleep in the nice clean hay in my stable tonight, since the inns are full." They didn't dream that Mary was going to give birth that night to her firstborn son, our Lord!

Set your figures of Joseph and the baby Jesus in the manger beside Mary and move the angel a little toward the back. If you used a picture last week, maybe you'd like to change it for a picture of the holy family. Enjoy the scene you have made.

Pray: "O God, our Lord, thank you for Jesus who came to the world to teach us how to be loving and caring. Help us to keep this spirit in our hearts all through the year; and even after Christmas, remind us to serve others in kindness and joy. Amen."

Sing: "Silent Night" or "Away in a Manger" or another favorite carol.

Legend of
The Christmas Carol

If a legend is a story based on truth, I suppose we could say that the song that the host of angels sang to the shepherds that night near Bethlehem was the beginning of our Christmas carols. What a choir that must have been!

In the days of the early church, when people changed from their old faith to become Christians, they had a great deal to learn about the life and teachings of Jesus. Luke's Gospel told them the story of God's gift of a Baby, born in a manger, who would become the Savior of the world. He told about the beautiful, brave young mother, Mary, and Joseph, the father who took good care of them. He wrote about the shepherds in the fields and the singing angels. These are the stories our Christmas carols tell and we still sing them today.

History tells us about a pope named Telesphorus who wrote some fine Christmas music for the church. In his time it was against the law to be a Christian. In spite of the threats of the Roman officials, Telesphorus decided that all church members should learn to sing. He composed a tune for the words "Glory to God in the Highest" and taught the people how to sing it in their native language. You can imagine what joy it brought to those persecuted Christians. But the officials meant what they said and in A.D. 137 the Pope Telesphorus was killed for his courageous faith. The church has honored him by naming him one of the martyred saints.

Early in the fourth century it was decided to make December

25 the celebration day for the birth of Christ. Persecution had ended. Priests were allowed to stroll through the villages and towns and sing hymns teaching the Christmas story.

By the thirteenth century, all the church members—not just the priests—wanted to sing. Christians in all kinds of situations—in humble work places, in schools, and in castles—began to sing carols about Jesus' birth. It was a good way for people who couldn't read and write to learn the Bible stories.

Later in this book you will read about Saint Francis and his live Nativity scene in Assisi, Italy. You also ought to know what this practical-minded pastor did about singing.

Even when people went to church, they didn't understand much of what was going on. They stood in a great crowd and only the tallest people could see what the priests were doing or hear what was being said. The Bible wasn't written in their common language and not many of them could read or write. Francis and his fellow monks made up songs that told the stories of the Bible, especially about the birth of Jesus and his life, death, and resurrection. Then these monks wandered from town to town, singing the story of the faith in language the people understood. They taught the people these popular tunes and gathered them together to sing. Before long there were carolers in every village!

This kind of carol singing spread from Italy to France, and then to Spain and Germany. The carols were always religious, easy to understand, childlike, and happy. It wasn't long before wandering minstrels carried the idea across the English Channel to Britain.

When we sing carols this Christmas season, let us think of all the people, in nearly 2,000 years who have helped bring them to us, and give thanks!

Legend of
The Little Drummer Boy

The Christ child lay safe in his little bed in Bethlehem. People came from far and near to worship him. They brought gifts of every kind. Some were simple things that made his mother, Mary, smile and some were beautiful and precious.

One day the Little Drummer Boy came, too, and stood back to watch the people going in and out. He saw the gifts they carried in and left beside the Baby and it made him very sad. He was only a little boy and he was poor. He wanted to worship the Christ child, too, but he didn't have a thing to give.

Although he was only a little boy, he did know how to play his drum. Sometimes he made believe that he was a soldier and he played as if the Roman centurions were marching by. Sometimes he drummed softly and sweetly as if he were playing for a wedding, and then he finished with merry tunes as if the whole village were dancing. Once in a while he imagined that he was playing for a funeral and tapped his drum in slow, sad beats. Other times he played happy, skipping tunes for the children where he lived. He even knew a lullaby song that he often played when his baby sister was fussy and couldn't go to sleep. But he didn't have a gift for the Christ child and he was very sad.

Suddenly a happy idea came to him and he smiled. "I haven't any gift," he said to himself, "but I can give the baby Jesus what I do have. I'll go in and play my drum!" He waited until all the big people had gone, then quietly he slipped in and stood beside the manger. At first he had to wait until his eyes got used to the dimness, and then he saw the beautiful Babe, wrapped in a cloth and lying on fresh, clean straw.

He tiptoed over to Mary, Jesus' mother, and whispered, "I haven't any gift but I'd like to play a little song if you think it's all right." The mother smiled and nodded. The little boy played his drum with all the love that was in his heart. He played his soldier tunes twice, his wedding song, his slow, sad funeral steps, and the children's play tunes, too. And then he played the lullaby. All the time he was playing, the animals were keeping time with him, nodding their heads.

The Christ child listened to the drum and clapped his hands in delight. When it was all over, he even held out his tiny hand to the Little Drummer Boy and smiled. Then the Little Drummer Boy knew that when you give the only thing you have with all the love in your heart, it turns out to be the very best gift of all!

Legend of
Saint Nicholas

Santa Claus has many other names, even some of which you have probably never heard. In Great Britain he's called "Father Christmas," in France his name is "Le Père Noël" (which means the same thing), and in Germany he's "Kriss Kringle."

Only in America does this gift-giver look like a "jolly old elf" who makes us laugh in spite of ourselves whenever we see him. He is roly-poly and wears a red suit trimmed with fur. In northern Europe and England he is tall and thin, wearing a long robe and riding a white horse. His special day is December 6.

You would be surprised at the number of people who call Saint Nicholas their "patron saint," meaning that he's their favorite saint to whom they pray. He is the patron saint of the people of Russia, sailors, children, bankers, students, pawnbrokers, and even vagabonds and thieves. They believe that he can help them anytime. There are legends which tell us why all of these people love him and think he looks after them in trouble. But I only have time to tell how he came to be one of the gift-bearers at Christmastime.

As with many historical characters, we know a few facts about Saint Nicholas. He lived in the first half of the fourth century. He was so young when he was elected a bishop of the church in Myra (a coast town in Lycia which is now part of Turkey) that they called him the "Boy Bishop." He probably suffered through at least one of the Roman persecutions. It is said that in the Middle Ages more people prayed to him than to any

other saint except Mary. Of course, they prayed to Jesus more than to any of the saints. Saint Nicholas was quite rich but he didn't spend money on himself. When he gave money away, he wanted it kept a secret. Listen to this popular legend which tells why he is our favorite gift-giver.

Once upon a time a father and mother had three daughters. The parents could hardly provide enough food and clothing for their girls as they grew up.

"What are we going to do?" asked the mother one night. "Paulita is old enough to marry now but no one seems to come courting."

"I've been worrying about that," answered the father. "All these years we've barely managed to keep alive. We haven't an extra penny saved, and a husband expects his bride to bring sheets, towels, tablecloths, and enough clothes to last for several years, plus money to help buy a farm or a house as well. What can we do?"

"I've taught her all she needs to know about housework, gardening, and the barn animals. Paulita is strong and healthy and she'll make a good wife, but no one will take her without a dowry." ("Dowry" is the word for the things a bride was supposed to give her husband.)

"In two more years Drusilla will be ready for marriage and after that comes Lucretia. They're not babies anymore; they eat as much as we do. We'll never be able to feed five grown-ups. Maybe we could sell one of the girls as a servant or slave."

"Never! No, never!" cried Mother, and they wept together and prayed for a long time.

Now the legend says that someone told Nicholas about this family. One night he crept up to the poor farmer's house and tossed a bag of gold into the open window.

"What's this!" cried the frightened mother as she picked up the bag that lay at her feet.

"Open it and see," urged Father.

The three maids crowded around as Mother, with trembling fingers, untied the string and poured out a heap of gold coins. They were all so excited that they didn't notice the note tied to the bag. Then Father opened the parchment and read: "This gold is a dowry for your lovely daughter, Paulita. May she find a good husband and make him a happy, loyal wife. I pray for you."

"It's not signed," exclaimed Lucretia.

"Who could have sent it?" wondered Mother.

"Well, someone meant for us to have it so Paulita could get herself a husband and a home. I say, 'God bless him, whoever he is!'"

When Drusilla was old enough to marry, Nicholas secretly left a bag of gold for her. When Lucretia's turn came, he did it again. But the third time the father discovered Nicholas just as he was tossing the bag of gold into the house.

"So you are the one, kind Bishop, who has helped me provide husbands for my daughters!"

"Shhhh! Please don't give me away," Nicholas whispered. "Promise you won't tell anyone until after I am dead!" Of course, the father promised.

Can you see why the church calls Nicholas a saint and why we love him still? "Santa" is just another spelling for "saint" and "Claus" is the Dutch way of pronouncing the last part of his name, "Cholas." When these words are pronounced they sound like "Santa Claus."

Have you ever given a secret present to someone who couldn't thank you? It's a lovely feeling.

Legend of
The Donkey's Bray

Surely you remember the story of Joseph and Mary fleeing from Herod's soldiers to save the baby Jesus' life. When King Herod heard about the birth of Jesus, King of the Jews, he was angry, jealous, and afraid. "*I* am the King of Israel!" he shouted. "No one else is ever going to be king!" He called his soldiers together. "Ride out and find every single baby boy in the country who is under two years old," he ordered, "and kill them all. That will take care of the new Baby King!"

Mary and Joseph were happy in Bethlehem with the Baby. They often talked about the wise men who had come and the rich gifts they had brought. But something they had said made Joseph uneasy, though he didn't know why. One night Joseph dreamed that God was telling him to take Mary and the Baby and leave Bethlehem at once. Joseph and Mary bundled up their precious child and started on their secret journey to Egypt the very next day.

That part of the story is true, as you know. There is a legend about this, too; but you will have to decide whether to believe it or not.

After Joseph and Mary had spent a long time in Egypt, they thought it would be safe to return to Nazareth. "I'll be so glad to be back in our home in Nazareth," Mary told her husband. "Yes," Joseph agreed, "and I'll be happy to get back to work in my carpenter shop. We've never been away for so long a time before."

Mary rode their little donkey, holding the baby Jesus, and Joseph guided them, walking beside. Every evening they camped just off the road, making a bed for themselves with their blankets on the ground.

One night the Little Donkey, who had very long ears, thought he heard something. He listened and listened. It was faint and far away but it sounded like horses' hoofbeats on the ground. Gradually the sound grew louder. He thought he could hear harnesses rattling and clinking as soldiers' heavy harnesses sometimes do. The Little Donkey was sure that Herod's soldiers were coming and would discover them and kill the baby Jesus.

Joseph and Mary were sound asleep, right out in the open under the stars, not far from the road. The Little Donkey knew he had to wake them up and help them find a hiding place behind the trees.

At that time donkeys had a gentle neigh, even sweeter than a horse. The Little Donkey neighed softly, but Joseph didn't hear him. He neighed again, louder, but still nobody stirred.

The hoofbeats were pounding nearer now and the Little Donkey was very frightened. How could he waken Mary and Joseph in time? He prayed very hard and then he neighed again. His voice came out in a great, harsh, piercing bray, surprising even himself! The holy family woke up! They barely had time to hide before the soldiers went clopping and clattering past. The baby Jesus was safe once again!

If you listen to a donkey bray these days, you will notice that his voice is harsh and shrill. But whenever he brays you will be reminded of his devotion to the Christ child.

Legend of
The Christmas Candle

Long, long ago, in ancient times, when people didn't understand about moons and suns and planets, they grew very frightened when they noticed that the days were growing shorter and shorter, as they still do every fall.

"What if the sun goes away and never comes back?" they wondered. "We will never be warm again."

At the beginning of winter some wise teachers noticed that the sun had begun to stay a little bit longer each day. They decided to have a great celebration. They called it "Saturnalia" because "Saturn" was the sun god's name. They lit many candles and thanked the gods for letting warmth and light come back to the world.

Jesus was born and lived and taught many years after the first Saturnalia festival. People who had always celebrated Saturnalia now became Christians and no longer believed in worshiping the sun god. But they remembered that Jesus had said, "I am the light of the world" (John 8:12). Because of this they joined in the celebration of lights with the other city people. Ever since, Christians have worshiped with lights of many kinds, especially on Christmas Day.

All over the world people put candles in their windows on Christmas Eve. According to some people, the first person in America to use candles in his window on Christmas Eve was Arthur Shurtleff, of Boston. He put a candle in his front window on Beacon Hill and soon windows all across the country were lighted at the Christmas season.

I think every child in Austria could tell you the following legend.

On the edge of a village there lived a poor shoemaker and his wife. Their cottage was very small and they had little food or clothing, but whatever they had, they shared with neighbors and friends or anyone who traveled their way. When it grew dark after sundown, they placed a lighted candle in their window so a wanderer could find their home. People who saw it understood that it meant, "Come in! We will help you if we can!"

This little village was just like all other villages everywhere. Sometimes there was sickness, famine or floods, storms or war. The cobbler and his wife tried to help wherever they could— and the strange thing was that none of these troubles ever seemed to happen to them. The neighbors wondered about it.

"There is something special about them," they whispered. "They don't seem to suffer like we do. Do you think it is because they put that lighted candle in their window every night? Let's all put candles in our windows and see what happens!"

The very first night that the neighbors put lighted candles in their windows was a Christmas Eve during wartime. Before Christmas morning even dawned, a special messenger came riding into the village. He shouted in a loud voice, "Praise God! Peace has been declared! The war is over and our soldiers will soon be coming home. Praise God!"

The village people could hardly believe it. They hurried to the church to give thanks for the blessing of peace on Christmas Day. They were amazed and awed at what had happened.

"It must be a miracle," they whispered to one another. "We will never forget to put lighted candles in our windows on the night of our Savior's birth!"

Legend of
The Christmas Bell

The Little Blind Boy was sitting on a big stone at the edge of the road, quietly resting. He really didn't have anything to do or anywhere to go or anyone to lead him that wintry afternoon. His little playmates had gone off to explore a cave and didn't want to take him because he might get hurt. His parents wouldn't be coming home from their work for another hour or two. But he didn't mind.

The Little Blind Boy liked sitting by the road and hearing the footsteps going by. He liked to listen and wonder who was passing and where they were going. It was a game he played alone.

But today the footsteps didn't sound like they did on ordinary days. There were many more than usual and they seemed to be hurrying and all going in one direction. There was excitement in the air as if something strange and mystical had happened.

The Little Blind Boy grew curious. He tried to hear what the hurrying persons were saying.

"The shepherds saw a great light and heard hundreds of voices singing praises to God!"

"An angel told them to go into Bethlehem and find a baby, wrapped in swaddling clothes, lying in a manger!"

"Half of the shepherds are staying with the sheep and we are going to find the Baby."

All these things the Little Blind Boy heard.

"Oh, I want to go, too! Please take me with you," cried the

Little Blind Boy, but no one heard. "Please, someone, please show me the way! I want to find the Christ child and worship him, too!" he called out, over and over. But the crowd was so eager to find the Baby in the manger that no one stopped to listen to the boy. No one noticed the Little Blind Boy, seated on a stone at the edge of the road.

Most of the crowd passed by and it grew quiet. Then the Little Blind Boy heard a faint tinkling sound. It sounded again. The Little Blind Boy listened with his very keen ears. It sounded like a bell! Yes, it was a bell, the kind sheep and cows wear around their necks to tell the shepherds where they are.

"Maybe the bell is on a cow or a sheep in the stable where the Baby is," he thought.

Slipping carefully down from the rock, the Little Blind Boy walked slowly toward the sound of the bell. Sometimes he had to stop and listen until the bell rang again and then he would follow it farther.

It wasn't long before he found himself in the stable, standing beside the animal with the tinkling bell. He reached his hands and felt the animal all over. It was a big, kind cow. When the cow felt the hands of the Little Blind Boy around his neck, he nudged him over to the place where the baby Jesus was sleeping in the manger. Then the Little Blind Boy knelt down and reached out to touch the Christ child and bless him with his prayer. "Thanks for the kind, big cow and his bell which helped me find the way," he prayed.

Bells have always rung out the glad tidings of Christ's birth. By the Middle Ages, around the years 800 to 1200, the pealing of bells was the main event of the Christmas celebration. In Italy it is traditional to wait for the bells to chime before lighting the candles and beginning the festivities.

The bells that ring out from every tower and steeple all over the world tell the message of God's love coming down to earth on Christmas Day. Do you imagine that the Little Blind Boy may have started it all?

Third Sunday of Advent—
Angels and Shepherds

A Service for "The Candle of Adoration"

As you come to your special Advent worship table, bring your little shepherds and sheep, or a picture of the shepherds adoring the Christ child. Do you have your Bible open to Luke and matches to light the candles?

Talk about the first two candles that you lighted and what they stood for; then light them once again. While you are lighting them repeat, "I light the Candle of Waiting," and "I light the Candle of Joy."

Sing: "The First Noel" or another favorite carol.

Read the Bible story: Luke 2:8-20.

Light the third candle of Advent, "The Candle of Adoration."

What a sight the shepherds on the hillside must have seen as they sat quietly beside their campfires! Their flocks of sheep were huddled down, sleeping around them. Each shepherd knew his own sheep by name. Around the outer edge the sheep dogs were on guard. Sometimes the shepherds sang and played their flutes like David did when he was a shepherd boy alone in the hills.

All of a sudden the shepherds heard many, many voices singing like angels! The sky was all aglow, brighter than the brightest moonlight. The voices were praising God and saying, "Go into the town and find a newborn Baby, wrapped in a cloth and sleeping in a stable. He is your Savior, Christ the Lord!"

What a surprise! When the songs and lights had gone away, someone said, "Let's go!" But someone else questioned, "Who

65

will guard the sheep? We can't leave them alone for the wolves to kill!" Maybe they argued back and forth for a while until someone said, "We could take turns going to see the baby Jesus; it isn't far to Bethlehem."

After they had reached an agreement, the shepherds went and found everything just as the angel had said. There must have been a special look about the Baby because the shepherds fell on their knees and worshiped him. Then they went back to tell the others all about it, singing the entire time.

Prayer: "Dear God: We're glad that the shepherds were not too frightened to go and see what had happened, so they could tell Luke about it and he could write it down for us. Help us to listen for holy voices that show us how to worship you. Help us to sing praises and spread the Good News to our families and friends. Amen."

Sing: "While Shepherds Watched Their Flocks by Night" or "O Little Town of Bethlehem."

Now place your shepherds, kneeling or standing, beside the manger with a few sheep nearby. Stand back and take a look at the scene you are creating week by week. Do you like it?

Legend of
The Mistletoe

Long before Jesus was born there were people called "Druids," who lived in England. You've read in some of the other legends how ancient people noticed that the sunlight grew shorter and shorter in the fall until they were afraid it might go away altogether and never come back. Then they would always have nighttime and there wouldn't be any sunshine to warm them. When the wisest people saw that at last the days were getting longer, a little every day, they decided to have a big holiday celebration for the sun. The Druids were among the ancient peoples who had experienced this.

The Druids also said to their children, "Do you see that vine way up there in the oak trees? It is a sacred plant. Once upon a time a mistle thrush came down from above and brought it to us. It was a gift from heaven. You must always respect it because it heals diseases and brings good luck!"

"And Grandma says it even protects us from witches," little Jan's voice added.

During the dark days of early winter when the sun stayed in the sky just a little longer, the Druids held their celebration. All of the people stood along the road to the forest to watch the priests come past in their long, white robes. Then they followed the procession to a big clearing under the sacred oak tree. They formed a huge circle and the priests stood under the tree.

"What are they doing, Father?" asked the youngest child.

"They are holding out those big white sheets under the tree

so that none of the mistletoe will fall on the ground. Watch and see!"

The chief priest climbed way up in the big branches of the sacred oak. He took a golden sickle and cut many mistletoe branches and dropped them carefully onto the white sheets so they couldn't touch the earth. Then he climbed down.

"What's he doing now, Father?" Jan wanted to know.

His father held Jan up on his shoulders so he could see everything.

"Do you see those two white bulls? The priests are sacrificing them and some mistletoe to the gods as a present. When the service is over they will give every family some mistletoe vines to take home. We will hang them over the doorway to bring peace and good luck."

"I don't see how a sprig of green mistletoe can bring peace and good luck."

"Be still, now, and watch! If any of our enemies meet under the mistletoe, they will throw down their spears and arrows and hug each other. That is peace. And if any of our neighbors are angry about something that happened this past year, we will stand under the vines and ask forgiveness and kiss each other and promise to be friends. That is peace. Even young lovers who kiss under the mistletoe will be happy and have good luck!"

Jan and his father followed the procession of priests and village folk back home, carrying their mistletoe branches carefully. Then they decorated their doorway with the branches and enjoyed their feast.

Years later the Druids were gradually converted to Christianity by courageous missionary monks, but the new Christians were afraid to give up their old beliefs in the sacred mistletoe with its leathery green leaves and its waxy white berries. So the Christian monks taught them that the mistletoe was a connecting link between earth and heaven since it grows in trees and never touches the ground. They hung wreaths over their church altars, believing that mistletoe stood for the healing power of God. When they gave the "sacred kiss of peace" in their Communion services they stood under a mistletoe wreath.

Not too many years ago people fashioned what they called a "kissing bough." It was a wreath of mistletoe with little fruits tied on it and a holy family tucked among the leaves. They put a lighted candle in it and hung it from the ceiling. It was a favorite decoration.

"We don't think mistletoe is religious or sacred these days," someone said, as I hung mine, with its silver bells and red velvet ribbon, in a doorway.

"No, it's just a charming custom," I replied. "We still enjoy hanging some where anyone is sure to walk under it. Then a daring young man can catch a pretty girl and give her a kiss!"

"But we've forgotten that in the olden days the man had to pluck off a berry each time he kissed a girl and when the sprig was bare he couldn't catch or kiss any more girls," Grandma said. She must have been listening in. "We had lots of fun when I was a lass!" And she nodded her pretty grey head and smiled as if she had secrets galore, but no matter how much we begged, she just wouldn't say anymore!

Legend of
La Befana

If you were a child in Italy you would be waiting for la Befana—not Santa Claus—at Christmastime. Her name means "Epiphany" and she waits until January 6 (Epiphany Day) to visit the homes of Italian children. On that day there are Befana fairs all over Italy, especially in Rome. At the fairs you can buy whistles and little toy figures of la Befana. She isn't a plump, jolly old elf who laughs and has twinkling eyes like our Santa. She is old and wrinkled and looks a bit like the "Wicked Witch of the West." Poor old la Befana! But the children love her.

The legend tells us that one day the wise men came through the village where la Befana lived. They were lost and couldn't find the way to Bethlehem. They asked la Befana to come with them and show them the way, but she was busy sweeping her house. Besides, it was cozy and warm inside and she didn't want to go out in the cold on such a long journey. So she sent them away. She wouldn't leave her housecleaning to guide the Magi. Some stories even say that she sent them in the wrong direction on purpose!

The next day, la Befana began to realize what she had done. She was sorry she hadn't helped them, and even though the wise men had been gone a long time, she started out after them. She took some little gifts in her apron to give to the baby Jesus. She hurried as fast as she could and looked everywhere but she never found the wise men or the Christ child.

Ever since that time, la Befana has been forced to wander up

and down the roads of the world, still searching for the caravan of camels and kings and the holy family. This is her punishment. No wonder she isn't happy—for she has never found them.

Even now she is in such a hurry that she rushes right into children's homes and straight into their bedrooms, even in the afternoon! She fills the stockings of good boys and girls with gifts. But when she finds a house with bad girls and boys, she fills their stockings with ashes. She doesn't laugh and sing "Ho, Ho, Ho!" like Santa does. She grumbles at good children, cackles in a harsh voice, and shakes her long finger at bad boys and girls. All year long Italian mothers warn their children, saying, "La Befana will get you if you're not good!" It must be frightening.

There is another legend which says that the shepherds told la Befana about the wonderful happenings in Bethlehem, but she waited too long before she began her journey to see the baby Jesus. The star was gone and she lost her way and has been wandering around ever since. This Befana leaves gifts at *every* house, still hoping that the little Christ child might be inside. Some people even say she comes down the chimney, like our Santa does.

Legend of
The Camels

In faraway countries where there are miles and miles of dry, dusty deserts, people ride on camels. Camels are the right kind of animals for traveling across deserts because they can go for many days and nights without a drink of water. That's good, because there is hardly ever any water in the desert. There is a legend that tells us how camels became able to go without water for long periods of time.

The wise men studied the stars and knew a great deal about them. They lived in different countries but each one knew that a new star was going to appear in the sky at a certain time. When they had figured out what time and where the star would appear to be the brightest, they sent messages to one another saying, "Let us meet and travel together to the place where the star will be brightest and nearest to earth and see if we can understand what it means."

They met at a certain place with all of their servants and food and water. The camel bells made a lovely sound as the long, swaying caravan started toward the land where the star would be clearly seen. At first they weren't quite sure whether or not the direction they were traveling was the correct one, but as the days went by, the star gradually came into sight. It grew brighter every night.

Finally, as they rested one night, an angel appeared to them and said, "This star is the sign of a new king. He will be a great king who will bring love and hope to all the world. The star will shine brightest on the night when the king is born. You will find him by the star!" And the angel went away.

Now the wise men knew that they had to hurry, but their whole caravan was very tired by this time. The days were terribly hot and dusty. Sometimes the wind blew hard and the sand got in their eyes. The water was almost gone. In fact, there was only enough for the people or the camels, but not for both.

The wise men went to the camels and asked them, "Do you think you can keep on going without any more water?" The camels also heard the angel's wonderful news and they were eager to reach Bethlehem in time for the birth of the king. They promised to keep going as long as they could without water.

The camels speeded up their steps and hurried on toward Bethlehem. Night and day, without rest or water, the camels plodded on, guided by the star which grew brighter every night. They were exhausted when they finally reached the place where the star was brightest and closest to the earth. It was over the stable where the Christ child was born.

When the wise men went inside to worship the Baby, the camels fell on their knees, too, and thanked God for giving them the strength and courage they needed. Then they drank, and drank, and drank gallons of clear, cool water from the stable's watering trough. Ever since then, as a reward for their bravery, camels have been able to travel for long periods of time without becoming thirsty.

Legend of
The Rosemary

You have probably noticed that several of the legends included in this book are about events which happened while Joseph and Mary were fleeing toward Egypt. They tell us more than once how Herod's soldiers almost caught the holy family. The "Legend of the Rosemary," however, is a pretty story which mothers can enjoy because it shows how Mary took care of her baby just the way all mothers do.

The journey from Bethlehem to Egypt was very long and frightening. Joseph was the father and protector. He had to find the way, watch out for snakes and wild animals, and guide the donkey on which Mary and the Baby were riding. Every evening he had to find a safe camping place and be sure that they weren't being followed by Herod's soldiers.

Mary was the mother, holding the infant Jesus in her arms as they jogged along on the donkey. She nursed him, changed him, washed his swaddling clothes and blankets, and made sure that he was warm at night. As long as they were all together and safe, Mary and Joseph were happy.

It seemed as if the flowers along the road bloomed just for them. The lilac sent out its strong, sweet fragrance and the lily stood tall and opened her beautiful gold and white cup. Beside these beautiful flowers the plain, green rosemary was sad because she had no blossoms and no fragrance with which to please the Christ child.

One day when the holy family stopped to rest, Mary said,

"I'll wash out some of the Baby's clothes right here in this little stream and dry them in the sun." Joseph tied up the donkey and held out his arms for the Baby so Mary could do her work.

When the clothes were all clean, Mary looked all around to see where she could hang them up to dry. "The lily will break if I hang them on her," she thought. "And the lilac is so tall I can't even reach it." Then she noticed the sturdy little green rosemary bush. She hung the Christ child's clothes there in the afternoon sun and the rosemary trembled for joy to think that she could help.

The clothes were soon dry and as Mary gathered them she said, "Thank you, gentle Rosemary. From now on you shall have blue flowers, to match the color of my cloak. And you will have a clean, spicy fragrance so that people will always remember that the garments of the little Christ child touched your leaves and blessed them!"

Legend of
The Stork

Oh, look!" exclaimed Gary, "Look up there on the chimney top. Isn't that a bird in a nest?"

"Of course. And there's another one on the tip of that church steeple. They're storks, our favorite birds," pointed Hans. "My grandmother used to tell us that the storks brought babies but we know better now."

"Why do you like them so much?"

"Everyone in Northern Europe does. They're so elegant with their long legs and long curvy necks and their white downy feathers. They leave us in the fall and ride the air currents all the way to Egypt, then fly right down to South Africa for the winter. Sometimes they go as far as eight thousand miles away. We miss them. I imagine that's how the stork in the story found her way to the manger in Bethlehem!"

"What story?" asked Gary, "You know we don't have storks in America."

"It's not a true story, of course. Grandmother tells it to us every Christmas Eve. Sit down, and I'll tell it to you.

"All the birds and animals came to worship the Christ child on Christmas Day. One by one the farm animals knelt down; the sheep, the goats, the cows and horses, donkeys and oxen, even chickens and geese honored him. They looked and prayed and gave thanks and then went back to their places in the stable.

"Before long all the wild animals and birds came running, flying and hippity-hopping over the fields. When they came to the stable they filed in quietly and stood around the manger. They fell on their knees and worshiped the tiny King of Creation. Then they returned to their homes.

"Meanwhile, a very beautiful but exhausted mother stork flew in and came to rest on the highest place. 'Oh, I'm so glad it's not over,' she panted. 'I was afraid I would be too late.' From her high perch she looked down and watched as the last of the animals got up and left. She watched as Mary and Joseph covered their precious Baby for the night and lay down to sleep.

"When everything was quiet the stork came down from her very high place and stood beside the manger. First she thanked God for helping her to arrive safely and in time; she had come so far! She also praised him for sending the Christ child into the world to bring love and forgiveness to every creature. When she opened her eyes and carefully looked around, every single animal as well as the parents were asleep.

"She was a splendid bird, tall and white, with bright eyes full of motherly concern. She examined the ragged blanket around the Baby and saw how thin the straw was underneath. 'My goodness,' she thought, 'my own babies always have a warmer nest than that! I'll just make him a bed like I do for them!'

"The motherly stork pulled the soft, white, downy feathers from her breast and tucked them under and over and all around the Baby. She smiled as he snuggled down in the warmth and slept more soundly.

"Grandmother says that's why the stork is our favorite bird," finished Hans.

Legend of
The Christmas Tree

There are so many legends about Christmas trees that whole books have been written just about trees!

One of the legends tells about Saint Boniface, a missionary monk who spent his whole life in Germany trying to tell the people about Jesus because at that time they didn't know about God's love.

One day, in the year A.D. 722, Boniface happened to walk into a big forest grove. There he found a group of people worshiping a huge old oak tree. He wanted somehow to show them that an oak tree couldn't love them as God does. He preached them a sermon to tell them that a tree could not be a god. "This oak tree cannot protect you or help you or teach you what is good. This oak tree cannot love you or comfort you or give you courage." But the people didn't listen to Boniface. They kept right on praying to the huge old oak.

When Boniface saw that his words were not changing their minds, he took up a great axe and cut down the sacred oak. The people screamed and wailed and scrambled out of the way as the big tree fell to the ground. "You see," cried Boniface, "if I can cut down your tree with my axe, I am stronger than it is. How can it be your god?"

As Boniface watched the tall trunk fall, a lovely little green fir tree that had been hidden before came into sight. "Take *this* tree home," he told them. "This green fir tree stands for everlasting life for it never will lose its leaves and is forever green. God's

love is like that; it lasts forever, even after death."

This legend tells us how the fir tree became the special tree of Christmas. It was many more years, however, before the tree had lights.

Martin Luther was a teaching minister and loving father. One starry night he was walking home from a meeting, looking at the sky. He was wondering how he could teach his children about the stars and God's creation. He cut down a tall fir tree and carried it into his house. Gathering his children around him, he placed candles on the branches and lit them one by one, teaching them all the while about the stars in the firmament and the God who created them.

The custom of lighted Christmas trees didn't become popular right away, however. The idea of a decorated tree came from the Black Forest in Germany. Around 1800, in the wars under Napoleon, some Prussian officers saw a tree all trimmed and told their families about it when they went home. The idea spread to the whole village!

In America, like all of our other Christmas customs, the custom of the Christmas tree came with the immigrants who brought their traditions with them from many lands over the sea.

Charles Fallon was a German refugee who taught at Harvard University around 1830. His neighbors saw his decorated Christmas tree and copied it and before you knew it, the custom quickly spread all over the city of Boston!

In 1840, a Mr. Goodridge had a gorgeously decorated tree in York, Pennsylvania. He sold tickets "so that ladies and gentlemen might come and be amused by it."[2]

Prince Albert, who was born in Germany, married Queen Victoria of England. On their second Christmas together, in 1841, he presented a royal tree to his bride. You can guess how elegant that tree must have been.

Now we can hardly imagine Christmas without a tree trimmed with lights and decorations. I hope we remember, as we admire our own trees, that the lights stand for Jesus, the light of the world, and that the star, which led the wise men to Bethlehem, has the place of honor at the very top.

[2] Ashland, Oregon, *The Daily Tidings*, December 4, 1981, p. 13.

Fourth Sunday in Advent— The Wise Men Come

A Service for "The Candle of Loving and Giving"

As we come to our Advent worship table let us bring the figures of the wise men and some camels, a picture of the wise men and the holy family, some matches, and the Bible opened to the story of the Magi. ("Magi" is a word that means "wise men.")

Light once again the first three candles and remember what we have talked about since Advent began:

1. The Candle of Waiting—Mary and the Angel,
2. The Candle of Joy—Mary, Joseph and the Baby in the manger,
3. The Candle of Adoration—The holy family and the shepherds.

Sing: "We Three Kings of Orient Are."
Read the story from the Bible: Matthew 2:1-13.

In ancient times whenever a new king was born, gifts were given to him. It was a way of saying, "We pledge you our loyalty and honor you with these offerings." The church celebrates the coming of the wise men on January 6 (Epiphany) or the Twelfth Day of Christmas.

In the church calendar Advent is a time of preparation for Christmas itself. The church celebration of Christmas really begins after the midnight Mass or Communion on Christmas Eve. That is confusing because on the day after Christmas all the stores begin taking down their decorations. But the "Twelve

Days of Christmas" have just begun! In some countries the children have to wait until January 6 to receive their gifts. That day is called "Epiphany," which means "appearance."

Our custom of giving gifts may have begun with the wise men bringing their gifts to Jesus. You have just read Matthew's report about the wise men coming from the East. The Bible doesn't say that there were *three* men. It doesn't say that they were *kings* either, but from that one short line in Matthew, tremendous stories have been imagined. The three kings have even been given names and countries. Melchior, king of Nubia; Gaspar, king of Chaldea; and Balthasar, a black king from Tarshish. Even though the Bible doesn't tell us these things, we can think of them as beautiful symbols. Since the wise men were Gentiles (not Jews) we can say that Christ came for all humankind, and the naming of the countries can stand for all the nations and races of the world which God loves equally.

Prayer: "God, we are thankful for these Sundays of preparation. As we think about the wise men who rode across the desert for weeks, searching for Jesus, help us to want to know him, too. Riding their camels day after day, the wise men must have found the trip long and tedious but they didn't give up until they found him. Help us to keep our eyes on the star, too, the star of God's loving spirit. Amen."

Place the wise men and their camels in your scene. Then sit back and enjoy it.

Light the fourth candle of Advent, "The Candle of Loving and Giving."

Christina Rosetti wrote some lovely short poems. Perhaps you know of one where she asked herself what she could give to the baby Jesus. She wasn't a shepherd so she didn't have a lamb to give. She wasn't one of the wise men so she couldn't give precious perfumes or spices or gold, but she could love him, and give him her heart.

Sing: "What Can I Give Him?"[3] or some other favorite carol.

[3] Danielson and Conant, *Songs for Little People* (New York: The Pilgrim Press).

Legend of
The Poinsettia

The first United States ambassador to Mexico was Dr. Joel Robert Poinsett. He liked very much the beautiful Christmas plant that grows in Mexico and when he came home he brought a plant with him. Flower scientists named it "Poinsettia" after Dr. Poinsett. Mexican boys and girls could tell you a very old legend about how this flower came to be.

In Mexico it was the custom in every church, no matter how big or small, to place the figure of the baby Jesus in a manger near the altar on Christmas Eve. And every person in the village brought a gift for the baby Jesus to their church on that night. Perhaps they still do; I've never been in Mexico at Christmastime.

In one small village there lived a little boy who was very poor. He didn't have a single thing he could take to his church for the baby Jesus. It made him very sad, and he prayed for a way to show the Christ child how much he loved him.

As he walked along the path to the church he saw some dried weeds that he thought looked pretty. He heard an angel voice saying, "Pick the weeds and place them on the altar tonight as your gift." He obeyed the voice; at least he now had something to give.

When he arrived at church he went inside and stood still in amazement. His simple church was decorated with all kinds of ornaments and hundreds of flickering candles. He watched all of the people of the village as they went to the altar one by one

and presented their gifts to the Christ child.

When his turn came he walked reverently down the aisle to where the baby Jesus lay in his manger. The little boy knelt down and said a prayer. He looked at the face of the Baby with all the love in his heart and then he laid his bunch of dried weeds beside the other gifts.

Everyone said that what happened next was a miracle. Before their very eyes, the bunch of dried weeds turned into a beautiful flower! Its leaves all along the stem were a deep green. The flower itself was shaped like a star and it was bright red. It wasn't dead, but alive and magnificent! Every person held his or her breath but the flower didn't fade away. They looked in awe at the little boy who had laid it there. He knelt again and gave thanks to God because his prayer had been answered.

Ever since that night the plant has been called "Flor de la Noche Buena," or "The Flower of the Holy Night." It is usually in full bloom at Christmastime. In our country we grow millions of them. We like to have banks of them in our churches and then take them to our sick and shut-in friends.

Legend of Santa Lucia

Mommie, when will I be old enough to be 'Queen of the Light?'" asked Ingrid, a little girl in Sweden.

"Oh, not for a few years yet," her mother smiled. "The tradition says she should be the prettiest girl in the house or the oldest daughter, so you have a long time to wait. Even after Hansena gets married next summer, Edda and Gerda still must have their turns. But you can help them sing and serve the coffee and cakes, you know."

"I know," sighed Ingrid. After a moment she added, "Tell me again, Mommie, why do we choose a Queen of the Light at Christmastime?"

"Come, sit here while I make some more cookies, and I'll tell you the story," smiled Mother. It was a busy time for her.

"Of course you know that here in Sweden our Christmastide begins on December 13—Saint Lucia's Day. Her name means 'light.' She is our very special saint in Sweden, because of her bravery and Christian faith."

"Why, what did she do, Mommie?"

"It all happened so long ago, almost 1,700 years, that no one is sure what is true and what is not. When people believed in Jesus and his teachings, they tried to be like him. They tried to be kind and loving and help people who were sick or lonely or poor. They were called 'Christians.'

"The leaders of the Roman Empire said that it was against the law to be a Christian. When they found anyone who believed in Jesus, he or she was killed.

"Lucia was a beautiful young maiden and a secret follower of Jesus. She was rich and gave most of her clothes and money to help others. When she was told that she had to marry a young man who did not believe in Jesus, she was frightened and sad. On her wedding day she gave her whole dowry to the poor! (Her dowry included all of the clothes, household things, and money that her father had given her to start a new home with her husband.) Everyone was shocked that a lovely young bride would do such a thing and, of course, her husband felt shamed before all of his family and friends. The judges said she must die, and she was tied to a post and a big pile of wood was placed around her to make a fire. But I've been told that when they tried to light the wood it just wouldn't burn; in the end a soldier killed her with a sword."

"Oh, what an awful story, Mommie."

"Yes, it is but it also shows how brave Lucia was and how she stood up for her faith. Those were terrible years for Christians. We honor Lucia by calling her a saint, and on December 13 we have lovely festivals and candlelight parades in her memory in every town. The Queen of Light is chosen and she rides in a beautifully decorated coach with her friends. You'll be big enough to stay up and see it all this year."

"But why do we let Hansena be Santa Lucia at home?"

"It's a smaller, more personal celebration in honor of Santa Lucia. The oldest daughter wears a white or red robe. On her head she wears a big crown wreath with lighted candles all around it. Before dawn she goes from room to room, waking the members of her family and serving them hot coffee and cakes. I don't suppose anyone ever imagined we'd still be honoring this faithful young Christian after all these years!"

"Mommie, don't you think Santa Lucia is glad to see Hansena and all the other Queens of Light having such a happy time on her special day? I do." Ingrid hopped down and ran to watch her big sister making her candle wreath.

Legend of
The Gold and Silver Cobwebs

Mother was so busy! There was so much to do! She arose early and she worked very late but sometimes she was afraid she would never get everything done. When she finally laid down to sleep on the night before Christmas Eve, she felt a little better. She had finished baking hundreds of cookies and had put them away; she had finished the presents and had wrapped and hidden them; and she had trimmed the Christmas tree. (In those long-ago days the children were not allowed to see the tree until they came home from church on Christmas Eve.)

Mother thought it was the prettiest tree she had ever trimmed. She stood and admired it for a few minutes, enjoying its beauty. "Shoo, shoo! Get out of here and let me go to bed," she scolded, shaking her apron at the cats and dog. "You will see it all when the children do!" She locked the door and put out the lights. All she had to do the last day before Christmas was the final cleaning of the house and the preparation of the dinner.

The little spiders were listening at their cracks and heard every word the mother said. They had been waiting and waiting for a chance to creep into the parlor and see the tree, but they had never found an opportunity. "*We* won't be there when the children come," they whispered, "we won't be allowed. Maybe we can find a way to see the tree in the morning."

When morning came, however, you never saw such sweeping, dusting, and scrubbing in all your life! Mother and Auntie, with the big girls' help, went over and under and into every bit

of the house with their brooms and feather dusters, waxing, shaking, and setting it all to rights. The spiders had to run for their lives or be brushed to death! They were as sad as sad could be, hidden away in their cracks, behind the doors, under the stairs, up in the attic, and down in the cellar. They didn't dare come out or whisper to one another.

At last the cleaning was done and supper was over and cleared away. The family, all dressed warmly in their best clothes, had driven off to church with their silver sleigh bells ringing in the frosty night.

A great quiet settled upon the house. Eventually the spiders noticed the silence. Cautiously they crept out from all of the corners of the house from under the stairs and behind the doors, up in the attic and down in the cellar they came.

"I think they've gone," said the big gray spider. "I think we're alone in the house." They listened and watched for a few more minutes. "Follow me," the gray spider commanded. Then cautiously and expectantly, they all filed into the parlor.

Spiders love beautiful things. If you've ever noticed a spider web sparkling in morning dew, you know what I mean. The tree was so splendidly trimmed with lovely things that it made them gasp. They had never seen anything so exquisite. Gradually they moved closer. They wanted to see and enjoy every single thing. Those appreciative, artistic spiders walked up and down and around the tree, from branch to branch, examining every pretty thing. At last, completely satisfied, they crept away to their hiding places.

Now, before the family came home, the Christ child came to bless the tree as he always does. Can you imagine! When he looked at it, he saw that it was criss-crossed with cobwebs from its star-tipped top to its lowest branch. The Christ child thought the silken webs were beautiful, but he knew how the tired mother would feel when she came home if after all her days and weeks of work she would find her best-ever tree all covered with cobwebs!

The Christ child lifted his hand, ever so lightly, and blessed the tree. The cobwebs turned to strands of gold and silver of dazzling beauty, from floor to ceiling.

That is why to this day we trim our Christmas trees with sparking garlands of gold and silver!

97

Legend of
The Little Juggler

The Little Boy stood across the street, watching. Person after person came around the corner and went in to see the baby Jesus. The Little Boy couldn't see what was going on inside for it was dim beyond the doorway, but he noticed that each person who went in carrying a gift came out with empty hands. The Little Boy decided that all those who went in to see the Christ child were showing their love for him and were worshiping him.

The Little Boy felt sad. He wanted to go inside and kneel before the tiny Babe, say his prayer, and leave a gift. He even imagined how the Baby would smile at him when he laid his present beside the crib. But the Little Boy had nothing to take; he just stood and watched.

All of a sudden the Little Boy's hand touched his favorite playthings in his pocket: three round sparkling balls which were very precious to him. He loved to toss them in the air and catch them again. They were red, yellow and blue, all shimmering in the sunlight.

"I'll go in and juggle for the Baby," he thought excitedly. He skipped across the street and into the dimly lit room.

As soon as his eyes were used to the darkness, he politely pushed his way through the people until he stood beside the Baby's crib. Then he began to juggle the brightly colored balls. The yellow, red, and blue seemed to sparkle mysteriously in the dim room. He knew that he had never juggled so well before.

The baby Jesus smiled! All the people stood back to watch

and clap. They had never seen a little boy juggle quite so well. And they remembered it for a long, long time—they even told their grandchildren about it!

The Little Boy whispered to the mother, Mary, "I wanted to bring him a gift and please him, too, but I didn't have anything to give."

"Your juggling is a gift of love," the mother whispered back. "The best gifts are the gifts of our hands."

And that is why we hang shiny, sparkling, colored balls on our Christmas trees every year.

Legend of
The Crèche

I can hardly wait from one Christmas to another just to see the lovely Nativity scene in our church. Wouldn't it be interesting to know how this tradition got started?

In our books on church history we read about many popes who were named "Gregory." It doesn't matter whether he was the second or third, but one of the popes named Gregory, who lived in the eighth century, had a statue of Mary and baby Jesus made and placed beside the altar in his church. Within two hundred years most of the other churches had one, too. A little later someone carved a donkey and an ox and set them beside the manger. Three hundred years later almost every church in Europe had a Nativity scene at Christmastime. By the year 1400 people had carved figures of angels and shepherds and added them to the rest to make the scene seem more like the first Christmas.

Just one thing didn't look real. The manger wasn't made like a box where the oxen and donkeys ate their food. The baby Jesus was laid on top of a table and the people didn't think it looked like a real manger.

In the year 1223 a monk named Francis, who was a very practical kind of teaching pastor, was trying to discover some way he could help his people remember how it was on the night when Jesus was born. He wanted them to know the stories in the Bible that Luke and Matthew had told.

At last he had an idea! He asked a farmer to build a real but

tiny manger. Then he had some wood-carvers make figures of Mary and Joseph and the baby Jesus. He also asked them to carve shepherds and the wise men, and the ox and donkey. He filled the little manger with straw and laid the Baby in it. He had the figures painted in live colors, too. Then he asked all of the people to come and help him carry the figures into the church and set it up like a real event. They lighted candles all around it. The village people saw how the first Christmas must have looked and they knelt down and worshiped God and thanked him for his great gift of the Christ child.

When Francis was much older, not long before his death, he wanted to see and feel for himself what it must have been like to be there when Jesus was born. He was a great teacher and had a good imagination. He had a friend who was a farmer and he asked him to bring his real animals to the village square in front of the church. He asked a carpenter to make a life-size manger and set it there. He used real people for Mary and Joseph and the Baby in the manger. He had live shepherds, wise men, and sheep. It was just like a drama of the first Christmas night!

All the village people entered into the excitement. They brought their candles and lanterns and lighted them, making the night seem bright. Saint Francis sang the Christmas Eve Mass right there, outdoors, beside the manger scene that he had created.

Legend of
The Holly

Holly branches with their bunches of red berries are among our favorite Christmas greens. Perhaps the reason we like the holly so much is because the Christ child blessed it one night. At least that's what this legend says.

The wise men had been to visit Jesus. King Herod had told the wise men to come back when they found this new baby king, and tell Herod where he lived so he could go and worship, too. But the wise men were *really* wise; they didn't trust King Herod. They left their gifts and started home another way.

Perhaps the wise men told Joseph about their fears, for he was uneasy. One night he dreamed that God was speaking to him, "Take the baby Jesus and his mother, Mary, and leave Bethlehem as fast as you can."

The very next day Joseph took Mary and the Baby and slipped out of town. They traveled by day and by night, as quietly as they could. If they could only get to the border of Egypt, King Herod could not harm them. He wasn't king in Egypt.

One dark night Joseph heard King Herod's soldiers following them. He knew they couldn't run away because the soldiers had swift military horses, while they had only a little donkey for Mary and the Baby to ride. There wasn't time to find a hiding place in rocks or a cave. The hoofbeats were coming too close, too fast.

Not far from the road they saw some thick, tall holly bushes. Mary took the baby Jesus and whispered a prayer for his safety.

She wrapped him tightly in her dark blue cloak and hid with him beneath the holly branches. Joseph took the little donkey and led him around to the back of the bushes; and they both stood very still. Then they waited.

It was winter and in those days the holly trees always lost their leaves in the fall, but now, miraculously, the tree pushed forth its prickly green leaves, thick enough to hide them. It also grew long, sharp thorns to guard the holy family.

Herod's soldiers rode right past the holly bushes while the holy family held its breath and prayed to God for safety. The soldiers never even saw them hiding there.

Then the little Christ child smiled and stretched out his hand and touched the holly bush as if to say, "Thank you, little holly." Since then the holly never loses its leaves in winter because one night "it held the Christ child in its heart!"

We know another legend that says that the holly is a sacred plant because it stands for the crown of thorns. When the crown of thorns was pressed onto the forehead of the Son of God, the blood trickled down onto the berries. Until that time, holly berries had always been white, but then they turned red and have been red every since. They remind us of the suffering of Jesus and his love for us.

The prickly holly bush is called "he" and the smooth one is called "she." In England, in the old days, they used to play a game on Christmas Eve day. People tried to see which kind of holly was brought into the house first, a "he" branch or a "she" branch. That way, they said, you could tell who was going to be the boss of the household for the coming year!

I think I like the first legend best. Which do you like?

Appendix

Suggestions for the Use of
Legends in Devotional Materials

During the Christmas season people in church groups and in inspirational and social agencies are often asked to present devotional talks to people of all ages. There are many ways in which the material contained in this book might be used. Perhaps the following ideas will help you. I will not specify the type of group or age for which these suggestions could be used, in the hope that you will feel more free to be creative in your own way. Keep in mind that persons of all ages enjoy legends.

A devotional talk should be short when followed by an inspirational or educational address. If the devotional talk is the main part of the program, of course it will be longer. There will be as much variety in plans as there is in the personalities who create them.

I. In an attractive basket decorated with Christmas greens and berries, place a selection of items which illustrate the legends you have chosen. Use those legends which appeal to *your* imagination and for which you have been able to find symbolic figures.

Singing a familiar carol is a good beginning.

This might be followed by reading or reciting in unison the shepherd's story as told in Luke 2:8-16 or 8-20. (Among older groups you may be surprised to find how many can recite this portion of Scripture, probably from the King James Version. It was learned when memorization was a strong part of education.)

Now, one at a time, hold up each item from your basket and tell its legend. As you finish that story, place the figure on the table where all can see. (Passing the articles around may seem like a good idea, but people too often become interested in the one they are holding and miss the rest. Invite them to come up afterward and look at and handle each article.)

A prayer could express the thought that although these simple stories from ancient times are not factual nor scriptural, they all teach us lessons of unselfishness, dedication, peace, and love.

If you do not feel able to compose a prayer, there are many beautiful poems which may express your thoughts. The words of several carols are meant to be prayers in verse:

"O Little Town of Bethlehem," especially stanza 3;
"As with Gladness Men of Old," especially stanza 3;
"Away in a Manger," stanza 3 (not always included);
"O Come, All Ye Faithful," especially stanza 3.
Singing the prayer verse or another carol may close the period.

II. Using the same outline as in I, make the following changes. Before the meeting, select a few persons to read one legend each. The stories will be varied by the differences in voice. These readers may also hold the figure which illustrates that legend. As they finish, they could place their figures in or around the Nativity scene, on the mantle, altar, or under the Christmas tree.

III. Still using the basic program outline in I, you might want to close by having the leader, when finished, invite anyone to come up and choose the figure which spoke a special message to him or her. While holding it, the person could tell why that particular story was a delight or of what it was a reminder. Then the article could be returned to its place. All could thoughtfully participate in a final prayer and song.

IV. A retired Christian social worker sent this plan. Some of the legends were incorporated into a devotional program for a women's circle at her church. Different members took turns reading some of the legends. They were followed by appropriate Scripture passages.

We know, of course, that Scriptures are not available for most legends, such as The Donkey's Bray, or The Lamb's Woolly Coat.

But many verses referring to patience, love, fortitude, joy, peace, kindness, and generosity can be used.

V. From the same friend came the suggestion for sending these legends into the homes during Advent. Many churches have a weekly or biweekly newsletter which goes to everyone in the constituency. The pastor could condense the legends and include enough for the number of days between each issue. In homes where there are children and even where there are none, reading the legends every day could serve as family devotion or miniature meditation. Scripture verses and carols could also be included with each legend.

VI. The following program suggestions were prepared for a women's group in Canada. The theme was "December, the month of good tidings and great joy."
1. Introductory and educational facts about what Advent means and its historical background and customs.
2. Inspirational thoughts, probing each person's readiness for Christ's coming. "Advent is a season, not a day."
3. Reading several short legends.
4. Singing a carol or hymn.
5. Prayers.
6. Benediction (blessings on our Christmas celebrations) followed by the song by Christina Rosetti (see the Fourth Sunday of Advent).
This must have been a service filled with new knowledge, interesting facts, charming legends, and inspiration.

VII. The following program was planned for an all-church family potluck dinner, opening the Advent season. A young mother, schoolteacher and church volunteer, was the designer and leader. There was a wide variety in age and attention span to consider in the planning.
The evening opened with the singing of a carol and short talk about the meaning of Advent as a time of preparation. This does not mean getting ready for our commercial Christmas but the preparation of our hearts. She reviewed the Christmas story as told by Luke.

A) She had collected and used in the table decorations as many articles as possible which were mentioned in the legends she planned to use.

B) She provided paper and crayons for the children and asked them to draw pictures of things which reminded them of Christmas. As the evening progressed, the adults helped the children to compare the drawings with the content of their table decorations which represented the legends. In this way they could discover whether the pictures they had drawn illustrated one of the legends or told the true meaning of Christmas.

C) Since many stories and traditions have grown up in the two thousand years which have passed since the birth of Jesus, the leader then told some of the legends, using a few props to interest the children.

D) Prior to the dinner small booklets containing the legends had been prepared so that every family could receive one to take home. They were asked to use them to help prepare themselves for Christmas, that their families might grow in love and peace together.

The leader thought that if the program were to be repeated, appropriate Scriptures could be found to correlate with the messages.

One woman who received the booklet of legends rewrote them on cards in a decorative manner. She placed them around her home near objects which the legends mentioned. Her guests enjoyed reading them. (Other people have been trying the art of beautiful printing, or calligraphy, and might use this idea.)

VIII. Unpacking our Christmas treasures is perhaps the most meaningful part of Christmas to me. Each item, unwrapped from its tissue or cotton nest, brings back memories of other homes, other stages of my life, and other Christmases. Many of these decorations were made by family or friends who have been gone from this life for a long time.

As the Nativity figures, animals, tree trimmings, and precious traditions are tenderly unpacked, legends could be read to the children to enhance the items. This would be enjoyable for all of us as we examine, enjoy, and decorate our homes for Christmas.

IX. A Christmas treasure hunt in home, church, or organization club room would be enjoyable, entertaining, and enlightening for all age groups. Here are two ways to carry it out.

1. Hide in plain sight all of the articles and figures which represent the legends. The leader asks each person to find and gather as many as possible in a limited amount of time.

As the players sit down together, the leader asks for one figure at a time and reads the legend which it illustrates.

2. Another way to play this game is to number all of the figures and hide them in plain view. A printed copy of the legends is given to each player; each legend is numbered to correspond to the numbers on the figures.

Players try to find the objects, but do so unobtrusively so that they do not call attention to the items. When a player finds an object, he or she checks off the number on his list, then moves away from the figure and reads the legend. The figure is left where it is, in the hope that another player will discover it in the same way.

When time is called, each player is asked to bring one or two of the figures which are most appealing to him or her to the group. Players check to see who found the most items. Then persons share the items they brought back to the group and their corresponding legends.

This game, if used as an inspirational meeting, could close with prayer and carol singing. It is especially good for early teens and senior adults.

X. Church school teachers will enjoy planning a worship service with their pupils, using the legends. It may be very simple, for a small class or department, or it may be enlarged for a program to which parents and friends have been invited.

Preschool children could participate by singing about the gentle brown cow and using the simplest of the animal legends.

XI. Many of the legends could be told in first person, or dramatized in costume. A devotional service or a children's Christmas program could be planned around this idea.

Bibliography

Forbush, William, ed., *Fox's Book of Martyrs*. New York: Holt, Rinehart and Winston, 1965.

Gale, Elizabeth Wright, ed., *Programs for Advent and Christmas*. Vol. 3. Valley Forge: Judson Press, 1989.

Latourette, Kenneth S., *A History of Christianity*. Rev. ed. New York: Harper and Row Publishers, Inc., 1975.

Nevins, Albert J. M. M., *A Saint for Your Name*. Huntington, Indiana: Our Sunday Visitor, Inc., 1980.

Shotwell, Malcolm G., *Creative Programs for the Church Year*. Valley Forge: Judson Press, 1986.